I See, You See

NOAH'S ARK

by Amy Bauman
Illustrated by MADA Design, Inc.

Meredith® Books
Des Moines, Iowa

'll tell you of Noah who lived long ago. A good and kind man whose God loved him so.

Find the following...

2 black sheep

1 white dove

2 ladybugs

2 butterflies

1 Ark plan

2 mice

1 shepherd's hook

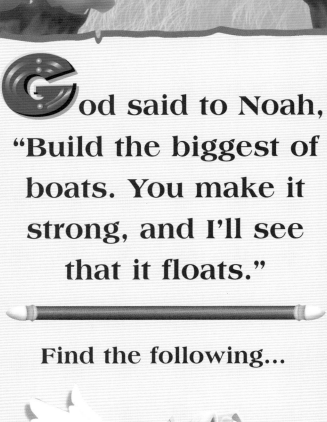

od said to Noah, "Build the biggest of boats. You make it strong, and I'll see that it floats."

Find the following...

1 white dove | 2 parrots

2 cats | 2 mice

2 neighbors | 2 sheep

1 hammer | 1 saw

Old Noah he listened and did as God asked. The neighbors, they hooted and doubted his task.

Find the following...

1 white dove

2 parrots

2 sheep

2 mice

2 cats

2 boys

2 pigs

1 neighbor

2 giraffes

When Noah was finished, God called him again. "Now gather all animals as fast as you can."

Find the following...

2 monkeys

1 white dove

2 parrots

2 cats

2 turtles

2 pigs

2 mice

2 snakes

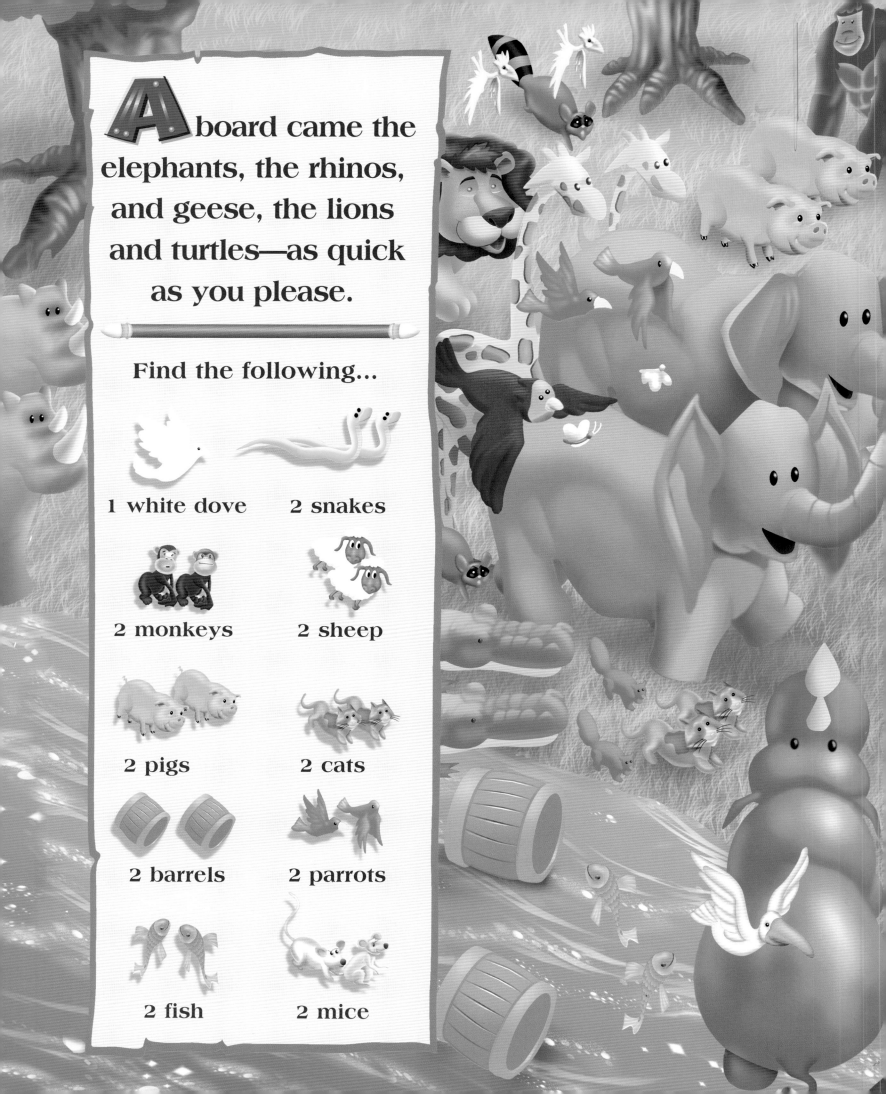

Aboard came the elephants, the rhinos, and geese, the lions and turtles—as quick as you please.

Find the following...

1 white dove

2 snakes

2 monkeys

2 sheep

2 pigs

2 cats

2 barrels

2 parrots

2 fish

2 mice

It rained forty days and forty nights too. While Noah kept watch on God's floating zoo.

Find the following...

1 white dove

2 parrots

2 cats

2 pigs

2 sheep

2 snakes

2 monkeys

2 mice

And then just as quickly the flooding rain stopped. The boat hit dry land; the gangplank was dropped.

Find the following...

2 toucans

1 white dove

2 monkeys

2 mice

2 kangaroos

2 bats

2 sheep

2 pigs

2 cats

2 snakes

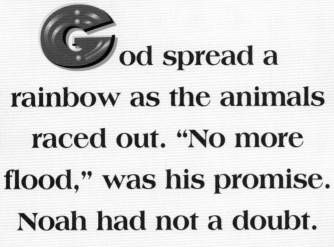od spread a rainbow as the animals raced out. "No more flood," was his promise. Noah had not a doubt.

Find the following...

1 white dove　　**2 snakes**

2 mice　　**2 sheep**

2 toucans　　**2 cats**

pigs &　　**2 kangaroos**
piglets

2 bats　　**2 monkeys**

How big was the Ark?

According to the Bible, God gave Noah specific measurements for the Ark. These measurements were given in cubits, an ancient unit of measurement equal to about 18 inches. By converting the measurements to inches and feet, it is believed that the Ark may have been more than 450 feet long and 75 feet wide. Since a football field is 300 feet long, you can imagine the Ark was huge.

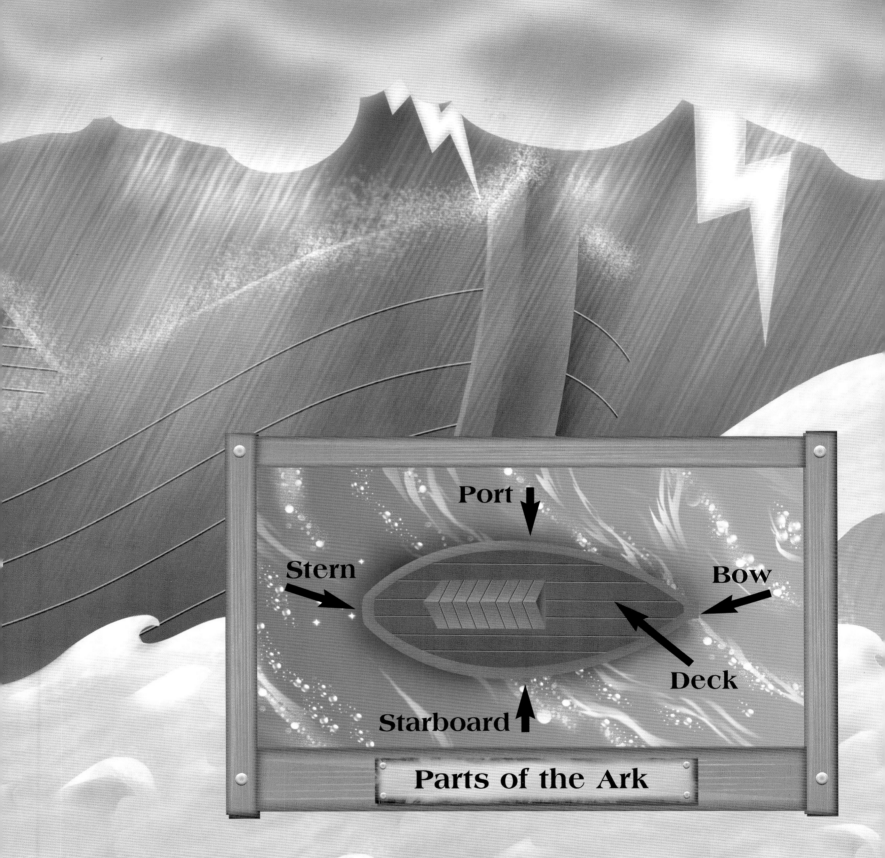

Parts of the Ark

Port ↓

Stern →

Bow ←

Deck

Starboard ↑

What is an Ark?

An Ark is a ship or boat. The term Ark is closely tied to the boat Noah and his family built to escape The Great Flood. The word, ark, comes from the Latin and Greek words that mean "to hold off, or to defend."

NOAH AND THE ARK

There once lived a man named Noah. Noah, his wife, and their sons—Shem, Ham, and Japheth—
were good people who loved God very much.
God knew this.

But God also knew that all of the world's people were not like Noah and his family. Many people
were living selfish, greedy lives, and this made God unhappy. So one day, God told Noah that a
great flood would soon wash over the Earth. God asked Noah to build a huge boat—an Ark, He
called it—that would safely carry Noah, his family, and two of every living creature through the
terrible event. It was a huge task, but God knew Noah could do it. So Noah and his family began
building the Ark according to God's plan and preparing for their difficult journey.

Many people—Noah's neighbors and even his friends—laughed when
they heard what Noah was doing. They didn't believe what God had
told Noah about the flood.

Despite what people said, Noah kept working, and, just as he finished, animals began to appear.
Two by two, the animals came: elephants, gorillas, snakes and cats, lions and giraffes, and
bears—and even butterflies! Two of every kind of
animal came to Noah, ready to board the Ark.

As the last of the animals climbed aboard, the rain began to fall. It poured and poured and
poured, lifting the Ark and sweeping it along on God's divine journey.